The Best c
Reel Fishern......

CW00584895

Dedications

Firstly, to our loyal readers and to all the contributors to the magazine over the years, without you this dream would never have been possible. Secondly, to all the anglers who enjoy this great sport, regardless of the species you fish for.

"There is nothing in the world more inspirational than a good story"

Introduction

Reel Fisherman was an idea born from the lack of angling material available nowadays, publications have disappeared from the newsagent's shelves quicker than a toupee in a hurricane!

Printed magazines are just one of the victims of the digital age where everything is so instant in todays hurried world, however there is still a dedicated following of print and so we have decided to compile some of the best articles Reel has had the honour of publishing and offer them in both a digital and printed format.

I believe there is nothing more inspiring than a story about a subject you are passionate about, I wanted to find out the truth behind some of the big fish that are caught each season by some of the most talented anglers in the UK. It is all well and good getting a snapshot on social media of a big fish, however, that is only part of the tale, very often the success behind the captures are interesting and eye opening. Specimen anglers put a tremendous amount of effort and time into consistently catching big fish from their chosen venues and they have kindly, within the pages of Reel, given up those secrets to our readers, going into detail about tactics and baits and most importantly, also relaying a good story along the way.

This book has been dedicated to the thousands of anglers that take to the banks every week to enjoy this fantastic hobby, some to find solitude, some to spend time with friends, others who seek out the bigger fish while others who are happy to catch whatever comes along, regardless of your incentive the fact that you are out there doing it, learning, practising and enveloping yourself within your surroundings makes you a passionate angler.

The committed angler will actively fish throughout the calendar, experiencing the four seasons in all their splendour and also their harshness, glorious summer sunrises, colourful days of autumn, frosty mornings of winter and the rejuvenating days of spring have all been well represented within this book. The ever-changing seasons offer the all-round angler new challenges keeping their optimism high, regardless of the weather there is always something to angle for, as has been proven by the contributors.

To catch big fish consistently the angler has to be dedicated and committed in his pursuit in targeting above average fish, not allowing a string of blanks to deter them from their goals, they are always learning and often trying innovative techniques to better their results. I regard the contributors in this book as some of the most inspirational anglers in the country, some are record holders, some are cup winners, however they all share the same passion for achieving their goals and consistently catching bigger than average fish, all doing this whilst holding down a full-time job!

We kick the book off with a man who has appeared on Sky Sports fishing programmes, a true all-round angler with several specimens of various species to his name, Colin Etherington. Colin fishes all year round and often keeps his approach simple, in the first chapter, Colin gets us all prepared for the pike season, talking about his approach in the entertaining style that he is famous for.

Dave Binns is an angler just as happy stalking barbel as he is mastering a pole for roach on the cut, Dave, often accompanied by his son Kyle, picks species dependant on the conditions at the time and opens his angling diary for us to reveal some extraordinary sessions and here he talks about big barbel.

Anto Roberts is well known for his barbel exploits on the river Wye, catching many doubles each season, however, this time he takes on an incredible journey onto an intimate estate lake in search of some stunning tench amidst the most beautiful surroundings.

After spending a large amount of time fishing and writing about big carp, Mark Dunwell is happiest fishing flowing water searching out barbel, chub and in this instance, The Lady of the Stream as he goes in search of grayling during those frosty winter days.

Dave Mutton is no stranger to big predators, he has travelled all over Europe in search of new adventures and his passion for perch, pike and catfish is second to none and Dave explains the advantages of lure fishing for predators at night in this eye-opening piece.

Big barbel and Jerry Gleeson go hand in hand, holder of several river records, Jerry has vast experience of both large and the more intimate rivers, here he goes into great detail about his preparations for targeting big barbel in his very unique style.

Dale Thomas, a true 'Erefordian, grew up on the banks of the Wye and decided to venture onto the bigger rivers in search of big fish, in this case it was carp with some very impressive results.

Vito Napoli is the true Chevin Chaser, preferring cane over carbon, Vito is also a fan of natural baits when fishing for barbel and chub and his list of big chub speaks for itself, this is not one to be missed if you love your chub fishing.

Gareth Thomas, ex sea fisherman, turned his skills to carp angling and has never looked back, with a string of big fish both in the UK and abroad Gareth fishes a variety of waters with great success.

Another committed all-round angler, Brett Longthorne is equally at home in search of zander or stalking big wily carp, however he is best known for his catches of big barbel and chub and here gives us the full run down on his tactics for catching those bigger fish.

Anthony Wood is an experienced angling author who works in the fishing industry and has a love of lure fishing, especially zander, with thousands of fish under his belt, he explains how to target them.

Personally, I have taken inspiration from all of these anglers and have drawn from their knowledge to help improve my own angling. This book has been designed to help and inspire other anglers, like yourself, to achieve their dreams and goals, a book you can turn to on those cold winter nights, a book that with every flick of the page triggers your passion, a book that will stir your emotions and a book that will galvanise your love for the sport.

The tactics and techniques described within these pages will also help you land that special fish, maybe that fish of a lifetime, there is so much to be taken away from these chapters that there is something for every angler regardless of your quarry, even if it is just the motivation to grab that rod and head for the bank, cast your line and relax, it is a book you will turn to time and time again. Tight Lines.........

Getting Prepared for Pike

Colin Etherington

If like me you aren't a one species angler then October always starts the season for piking. It is a great month to be out on the bank and most species can be caught regardless of the longer nights and shorter days. We should start to see the first frosts of autumn and the lovely foliage we enjoyed all summer starts to die back.

Underfoot we can feel the crunch of Jack Frost and we can start to see our breath freeze in the cold morning air as we head to our chosen swim. I can almost feel the excitement whilst writing this and cannot wait to get my pike gear ready for the new season.

Pike has to be one of the most exciting species to catch, as your float bobs and then disappears into the depths you just never know whether it's a big female or a small male jack that's picked up your bait.

The anticipation as you wind down before bending into the fish is simply awesome and then of course your rod takes on the arc of the predator and you get the first indication of the size of the pike.

As we move into September, I always start planning my winter campaign. Tench are slowly forgotten as the nights get longer but I do return to my tench lake in order to catch some roach and rudd for freezing down as dead baits. I'm fortunate to have a small freezer in my garage to accommodate my baits, it has been a great investment as my wife and children don't necessarily want my bait kept alongside their food. I normally do a couple of afternoons on the waggler or even just on a 3m whip to hand. Maggot tends to be my bait of choice and I can normally manage a 100 or so baits in a few hours. These baits are then separated into freezer bags with 5-6 in a pack before laying flat and frozen. I don't use huge baits either, I like to use 4-6" baits and generally prefer rudd over roach. Not all venues allow you to bring your own freshwater baits so, I always stock up my freezer with some sea dead baits too. These are a mixture of both sardines and joey mackerel. The mackerel I like to catch myself from the beach whilst major supermarkets are excellent places to source sardines. Although I don't practice this method all the time it can be advantageous to inject your baits with a fish oil, various options are available and it can be very productive in particular on rivers. The baits give off extra scents that your quarry can then home in on.

Once my bait is sorted, I then look at my tackle for the first time for over 6 months, it's been left alone in my garage and I always will replace my line. It is arguable as to whether this is necessary but I want to make sure that the cards are stacked in my favour if I hook a big fish. There is nothing worse than putting in the hours and then losing a fish due to a line breakage. Normally I will opt for 15lb breaking strain across all three reels and also clean down my rods with baby wet wipes. Most of my pike fishing is carried out at short range with rarely the need to overarm cast. Therefore, I'm nearly always float ledgering either a dead bait or on occasions the odd live bait. I've found over the years this is a very sensitive method and enables you to know exactly what's going on and as soon as any pike picks up your bait you get an indication on your float. In using this method, I also do away with the need of alarms and on occasions even bank sticks don't come into play. The floats I've acquired over the years have basically stayed the same and are a mixture of handmade wooden floats and clear plastic cigars. One of the added benefits of float ledgering is that you plumb around and get the depth exactly right giving you the knowledge you need in where you place your baits. Personally, I've always done well fishing the margins alongside reeds or against an old bed of lilies. The ledger weight I use is relatively light and is normally a 1oz arseley bomb with a bead used to protect the knot connecting my wire trace.

Once my rods are cast out and I'm happy, I will then cut up 2 extra fish into 1-2" sections and then will hand feed these around my hook baits. I'm convinced this gives an extra scent trail into the water thus drawing the predators to my baits. If I have any left-over maggots, I will also catapult a pouch full around the baits, I'm sure that getting any silver fish feeding also will have the same desired effect of gaining the interest of pike. Normally, I will give the rods an hour before tweaking the line back 6", on many an occasion I've had an instant take doing this. A decision can then be made to either move swim and cover more water or to recast and start the same process. Most of the swims I fish are relatively deep and I'm particularly confident when I have 6-10' of water straight off the bank in front of me. If my float is slightly over depth, I will engage the bait runner on my reels and tighten the line back onto the spool. This will tighten the line to my ledger weight and in turn cock the float. Bites are unmistakable and normally the float will bob slightly before disappearing under water, as soon as I get any indication on the float, I will pull two foot of line off the spool and as it tightens up, I then disengage the bait runner and wind down to the fish and set the hooks. This will nearly always result in a mouth hooked fish that is relatively easy to unhook. Targeting pike on short sessions means you don't need to bring as much tackle as you would doing a longer carp session, so travel light and make it easy to move swims.

I think confidence in your fishing is an absolute must and that goes for pike fishing as well, I'm very much a short session angler and consequently I need to maximise my time on the bank. I use my knowledge gained during the summer months to achieve this and will have noted swims that pike showed earlier in the season. It might have been a swim where I had roach attacked on the retrieve or where I've seen a continual scattering of fish. I'm also not adverse to pre bating a swim, however the effectiveness of this can be tricky to gauge. I don't like to over feed a swim either so if I decide to pre bait a swim I would use similar bait to my hook bait and feed small sections and half baits into likely areas I'm going to fish. It's important to feed these at the same time you are going to start your session as you don't want the fish to see it as a food source at a completely different time of day. If for example you are restricted to morning sessions introduce your freebies at dawn not for example at dusk. I'm not saying that if you follow this you are going to catch monster pike but you will see an increase in your confidence which can only stand you in good stead whilst actually on the bank fishing. You can also introduce some balls of ground bait laced with maggots and casters; this will in turn obviously draw in the silver fish which ultimately will mean the pike aren't far away. The classic saying "the sprat to catch the mackerel" springs to mind.

If something is working for you don't change it but if for whatever reason your method isn't working then now is the time to start changing things. Location of your chosen species is paramount to your success and this goes for every species you target. Don't sit in the same swims week in week out blanking, if you haven't had a take then move and eventually you will cross paths with the pike. Quite often during the winter months there are club matches on a Saturday or Sunday and these events are great for gathering information. I like to tackle swims that have produced well during the matches especially if lots of silvers have been caught. Where there's silvers there's normally a predator or two not far behind as they can be easy pickings for our intended prey.

Other tackle that is essential for your campaign comprise of a decent set of forceps, wire traces and of course an unhooking mat and big net. I'm not going to go into the art of unhooking pike in this article but if you are a complete novice, I'd suggest you either fish alongside an experienced angler or watch the many videos that are available online. Pike fishing is normally carried out during the winter months and consequently the temperatures can be incredibly cold. Therefore, please wear appropriate clothing as otherwise you simply won't enjoy yourselves. There is nothing worse than sitting on the bank with cold feet and hands, always take a flask of hot coffee or tea and be prepared to wait whilst sitting motionless. Quite often pike are right under your feet so don't cast your rods out too far and remember pike are the masters of ambush so fish alongside visible features.

Tight lines for everyone that are out and about on the banks this autumn.

Diary of an All-Rounder

Dave Binns

What a month of two half's September turned out to be hey, and in true all-rounder fashion my fishing reflected it. You may recall that at the end of my last piece I wrote that I intended to spend some time on the river Trent. Well, given the conditions at the start of the month, that had to wait. It was very low, gin clear and reports from the bank were not good.

The weather forecast was for warm, sunny conditions so we decided to see if we could tempt a late crucian or two from the club lake before sacking it off until next spring. I opted to fish the same swim I fished last time, purely because the wind was pushing into it as it was before and I knew the fish visited that area. Kyle dropped into the next swim, I had seen signs of fish here previously and the wind was also pushing into that one too.

My bait and methods remained unchanged and Kyle followed my lead, a method feeder on one rod and float fishing over small balls of ground bait on the other. It was pretty chilly to start with early doors and the fishing was also slow to get going with the small fish not being so ravenous which was a good thing. Just the odd small roach or perch were swung to hand in the first couple of hours.

Sport never really picked up the pace and no crucians had shown by the time the sun broke through and warmed us up a little mid morning. I could though see a trio of decent sized perch mooching around under the rod tip between the dying lily pads. Time for a bit of fun I thought and watched as they gobbled down the maggots I dropped in for them.

I baited my float rig with a small worm and lowered it between the pads, the fish showed an immediate interest but were clearly spooked by the shot on the line. I had been fishing with bulk shot to get through the small silver fish so I moved the shot up the line out of the way and lowered my worm back in. It was taken instantly by the smallest of the trio.

This spooked the others so I got back to fishing for the crucians and began picking up the odd small roach and rudd plus occasional skimmer. Kyle was fairing much the same with a few silvers keeping his attention levels up but still no sign of anything bigger.

A while later I noticed a big perch trying to bully the resident jack pike out of the way as I landed small silver fish. This one though wouldn't fall for the same dangled worm trick and when I again hooked a small rudd the perch actually tried to snatch it as a pike often does. That was all I needed to see and a plan was put into action. If it was up for chasing bait fish then I would give it one to chase.

The plan was to catch a small silver fish and lip hook it using my other rod and a much bigger hook. First cast in with my float rod and a perfect sized rudd came out of the water, unfortunately it dropped off as I tried to swing it to hand. The big perch appeared again and chased after it as it made good its escape. I re baited with double red maggot and cast back out to my spot just past the margin shelf.

My float settled before disappearing from view almost instantly. I struck and expected a small fish to be on the end so I was taken by surprise as my rod hooped over. I presumed it was going to finally be a crucian but after a five minute battle I was surprised to see a big perch appear in the clear margins. I guess it's the one that was chasing the prey fish but who knows. Anyway, best made plans and all that but I'll settle for that one especially as no crucian carp did show for either of us before we called it a day.

A few days later I had chance to do an evening on my local river after the barbel. It was low and clear and as it got dark the moon shone just as bright as the sun. The river seemed lifeless and I'd not seen any barbel during day light. As expected, it was another blank and not even the chub troubled me.

The following weekend I was back on the local river but this time hoping I could stalk some chub before the weed started to die off and they head to deeper water. I was also carrying a barbel rod just in case. It was a pre- dawn start and before it got light, I spent a bite less hour in a swim on the off chance of sneaking a barbel out. That wasn't to be and the chair was soon dumped back in the car along with my coat and off I went up river.

It was desperately low, so low in fact I don't think I've ever seen it like that. The weed was still there though giving the fish some much needed cover. The sun was up and burning bright in no time though and the chub were super spooky, so spooky that I couldn't even get them to feed confidently on loose fed pellet. Single fish would cruise in and intercept the odd free offering but that was all. The moment a rig was in the water or I free lined a bait near them they just spooked.

I tried a number of swims and they just wouldn't have it. I had seen no barbel either so headed home before dinner. That's the end of the stalking for this year and my chub fishing will now switch to bread, paste and worm fishing using a tip rod. The rivers are desperately low and clear and in serious need of rain. As I said, it's been a month of two half's and that much needed rain really did come with a vengeance.

For a week it rained solid and by the weekend the rivers were filling nicely with lots more to come, this coincided with big spring tides too meaning the tidal Trent was swilling the bank tops when myself and Kyle arrived on Saturday morning. The bulk of the flood water was still in the upper and middle reaches so once the tide turned, we could be sure that the river wouldn't continue to rise and cause us any issues.

We chose to fish an area on one of our club tickets that doesn't get fished much but does have good form in flood conditions for those in the know. It took us a while to find a spot to fish, the track was tricky in the car but there was also a lack of marked or used swims along this section. Eventually we found what looked like a couple of old swims that only required the nettles to be flattened down and were actually quite comfortable swims. I opted to fish the downstream one purely because the banking in the upstream one looked a lot safer for Kyle.

A quick chuck around before we got all our gear our revealed it to be largely clear and 5oz was holding well. I like to do this on new areas as it's better to find snags and such before getting all your gear out, set up, then finding you have to move.

First job was to get some bait out and for this I would use a spopper, if you've not got one of these then you really are missing a trick. I had brought along an old carp rod and big reel loaded with 20lb braid to attach the spopper to.

Our mix contained hemp, micro pellets, 4mm halibut and 6mm stimanol pellets and broken stimanol boilies. Ground bait was the ever-faithful Hook bait Co. Stimanol with a good addition of stimanol boilie crumb. I introduced 10 spoppers to begin with in both our swims and we were casting big feeders every ten minutes. We had brought along boilies and paste, flakey and spam for hook baits.

Within an hour of starting my downstream rod was away first and after a short tussle the first double figure barbel of the session was in the net having taken a large lump of spam.

High tide arrived and with it so did the bad weather and for around half an hour we were battered by strong winds and sideways rain. Thankfully our Korum brollys held firm and did their job. These Korum ones really are strong and hold firm so long as they are well pegged down. The strong wind continued after the rain had passed and as it was pushing upstream against the flow it was causing quite a swell on the river and nothing much was happening.

Not long after dinner conditions improved, the wind dropped and the sun even came out for a while and I introduced another six spoppers of bait in to each of our swims and not long after Kyle shouted up that he was into a fish. As I stood up, he asked if I would come and grab his other rod as the fish had set off down river at speed and gone under his line. By the time I got his rod in the fish was now past my rods and still going!

I told Kyle the best thing to do was to follow it down river as it would just get caught in the near bank scrub covered by the high water. He kept a tight line on the fish as he walked down stream, ducking under my rods as he went. I wound in my rods and brought my net along to the next swim down. The fish had now stopped running and was fighting hard in the flow.

After a few minutes, a very thick fish rolled before shooting off again. Kyle piled on the pressure though and after the fish made a couple of short dives it rolled onto the surface and I managed to get down the banking enough to scoop up a very deep looking fish. I looked at Kyle, Kyle looked at the fish and we both just looked at each other.

After it had had a good rest, we made our way to my swim as my mat was already out and the scales were in my bag. A short but very stocky fish had taken a combination of Hook bait Co. Nimrod boilie and spicy meat flakey. Into the sling it went and I think Kyle was expecting a new personal best but the fish fell just 4oz short recording a weight of 14lb 8oz.

Nothing else was forthcoming so I put in another six spoppers in each swim and decided we would stop till it got dark and we couldn't see the rod tips. Late afternoon and my downstream rod was away again, this time a paste wrapped Nimrod boilie had been picked up and after a good battle I netted my second double of 11 ½ pounds.

The light was fading and we had started to slowly pack our gear away, as always leaving the rods out till the last minute and I was just folding my chair away when I had what I though was a bream bite so finished folding my chair before picking up a slowly nodding rod. As I wound down it went solid and at first, I thought it was snagged until it started to slowly move around.

It was very weird, just a heavy weight not really doing much but obviously a fish. I was starting to think it could be a carp given the way it was fighting so I was a little surprised when another double figure barbel popped up on the surface and slid straight into the net. No obvious defects and hooked perfectly in the mouth, just a very odd fight.

That was it for the day, I didn't re cast the rod, just continued to slowly pack the rest of the gear away. It had been a great first visit of the season to the Trent and all being well there will be lots more fish to come over the next few weeks. The rain has continued to fall and as I type the river has just dropped back into its banks after being over them but it is rising again in the upper reaches.

Estate Lake Dream

Anto Roberts

Hidden in the south west of Wales lies a hidden little known Estate Lake, a place you can lose yourself, in awe of its unrivalled beauty and peace, I first became aware of it on one of my rural postal rounds, there were a couple of pools which I could see from the lane as I drove past the Estate each day on my daily round. Since I had resumed angling, I had only fished small commercial lakes and pools, but these pools had a different look about them, as if they had never been fished, a wild look, my angling mind started working overtime, what might lie beneath the hidden depths down the bottom of the field, I yearned to investigate.

Shortly after joining the local angling club I found to my surprise these were run by this very club, to my astonishment there was supposed to be a lower hidden lake, but where I thought, I could only see two, apparently there was a lake below these, the only access was through a field and a walk through a wood, after fishing the two obvious pools and catching carp, rudd and perch I decided to investigate this hidden lake, the access through the woodland was very overgrown, it appeared this lake hadn't been fished in a long time. After struggling through the undergrowth, wading through mud jumping over a stream as you journey through the dense woodland, finally arriving at the lakeside, you could understand why most anglers would not be interested in having to put this sort of effort in pursuit of their hobby, this sort of dedication is only found in serious anglers.

Upon arrival I found the swims and bank almost inaccessible, it looked like a place lost in time, the silence was eerie, it was not silence in the sense of the word, I could hear birds wildlife even seen a deer but no noise we are normally accustomed to, cars, roads, people, I couldn't have felt any further from civilisation, it was beautiful. After joining the club committee I had learnt that anglers who had to tried to fish the lake had been disillusioned after many sessions of blanking and were utterly convinced the lake was devoid of fish, how could this be, the lake was stocked in 2008 with tench and bream I was told, why were these very competent anglers blanking, it just didn't make sense. I decided to make the next trip with another member, the very member that went on to introduce me to barbel fishing at a later stage, he had told me he had never caught or seen tench or bream in the sessions he had tried, but there was one species he had caught, perch.

Ideally, I wanted a tench but a nice perch would be welcome, armed with worms and maggots we set on our journey, over the next few weeks we had very good sessions with them, one session that stays with me is when I caught eleven perch between 1lb - 2lb 8oz. The next session was to change everything, it was on a day when I decided to change swims because nothing was happening, I said to him I'm going to try a swim I'd never tried before, so off with my maggots I went to other side of lake, I dropped my float into the margin that lay in front of a wall of reeds and continued to feed in a few maggots every 2 minutes over the float, all of a sudden the float disappeared in a blink of an eye, I immediately struck into it, this was no perch, whatever this was, was much bigger, after a fight of about one minute the line went slack, I won't say what word was going through my mind but you get my drift, this had made up my mind, my next session I would start to introduce boilies while carrying on using a float rod with maggots or worm as well, I began to realise why the stocked fish were hard to catch, the lake was so weedy it was teeming with natural food already, if I could just get them accustomed to taking boilies perhaps I would stand a better chance, at that time another member Darren Davies, had been having a lot of success with a bait he had been testing, a sweet creamy flavour boilie, I decided to purchase some boilies for myself as tench are known for liking sweet flavoured corn and boilies, so with that I proceeded to bait up a couple of swims over the next couple of weeks, that decision I had made was the game changer, my first tench was around 3lb, a classic beautiful olive green, not big but a start.

Tench are a beautiful fish and can vary in colour from olive green to almost black depending on their environment and venue, a lot of commercial venues hold very pale looking specimens in comparison, the setup I used was a 1.75tc Barbel rod with scaled down carp style rig using a size ten hook the following sessions proved productive as well, they had taken a liking to these new boilies and on average I was landing 4-5 tench a session averaging 3-4lb in weight, I still used a float setup on the other rod but the scaled down carp style rod seemed to bag the bigger and most fish.

The lake didn't seem to be heavily stocked like your usual commercial pools or lakes, these tench were in pristine condition, this place was a jewel in the clubs crown, in a way it reminded me of Redmire because of its seclusion and wild look, like most anglers I began to wonder what size they went up to, for the rest of the closed river season I had caught nothing bigger than 4lb 8oz fishing the venue once a week on average, but one thing I was sure of, I would be back at the end of the river season, the following year I couldn't wait to get up there, it was towards the second half of April still relatively cold, it is thought by the handful of members who fish it to this day that the lake is a late starter and isn't fished until May by most of them.

I went up anyway thinking I can only try, I was so glad I did, it turned out to be my best session to date, landing 5 fish with the biggest two being 5lb and 6lb in weight, supposedly a club record for unspawned tench at the time, I had heard another member and friend Darren had caught it at just under 7lb the previous year prior to spawning, another record.

The remainder of the closed season was very good but I never got close to catching anything close to 6lb again that year, I had the 5lb out again and the usual average 3-4lb but was pleased I managed to get my PB, this year I hope to break it. This place makes the closed season very bearable, I love the place, there is nothing like arriving at your favourite location when the sun is rising and the morning mist is rising off the lake. It truly is the lake of dreams.

Frosty Mornings in Search of Grayling

Mark Dunwell

As an angler who spent a long time chasing big carp it's hard to lose focus on why I started fishing in the first place. I remember as a kid and much to my father's annoyance wanting to go fishing at 3am, every Saturday night felt like Christmas eve waiting to go fishing on a Sunday.

Changing from being a one species angler awoke the child in me once again, now as a near fifty-year-old man still feel the excitement I felt as a boy. That's what I believe being a multi species angler does for you. It's the change in the seasons that bring in a change of approach both in species and more often than not venue. When I finish a night shift this time of year nothing pleases me more than a good frost and a thin layer of ice on the windscreen. Thoughts of clear rivers and big grayling come to mind and a box full of maggots.

I feel myself lucky to live where I do in Yorkshire as I've several rivers all within a thirty minute drive, they may not hold the monsters of the Frome or Itchen but targets need to be realistic and two pounds is still a good fish from anywhere but certainly away from southern chalk streams is still a big fish nationwide.

All my fishing is quite simple, all fishing is, it's us anglers that make it complicated often we see a novice or new angler catch a big fish? The key is normally location and watercraft that means the odd accidental capture a regular thing. I was brought up on rivers before I turned to carp fishing and in particular the river Wharfe at Boston Spa, like most Yorkshire rivers they have everything from shallow rapid water to deep wide stretches, over a period of time you learn how to adapt your tactics given the nature of the swims e.g. depth, cover and weed. Species also change and time spent exploring the river is never wasted. Watercraft is something you learn from experience; you can read books and talk to anglers but nothing beats time spent on the bank. If you read all the magazines, grayling love fast flowing water over clean gravel but some of my biggest fish have come from deep bends that flow over sandy or slightly silty riverbeds. Fish have fins and like to move about I've seen my angling friends drop into swims we have blanked in several times and had a two pound plus fish. Being able to adapt and think outside the box is sometimes what separates the more successful anglers from the guy who always follows 'the rules'

Any approach to a new river is always the same, love or loathe social media it's a great place to start, angling clubs normally have Facebook pages and several groups are set up covering every species. The local tackle shop is always a great place to pick up little tips to get you started on location although the size of fish should be taken with a pinch of salt. Nearly every carp lake I've fished held a mythical fifty pound never caught common or park lake pike that eats dogs or small kids!

Time spent walking a venue is never wasted and winter gives you the ideal opportunity, clear water and the lack of bankside cover can make fish spotting easier than the height of summer when fish seek sanctuary under overhanging trees or dense weedbeds.If you see nothing be at the river at dusk even in the coldest conditions grayling or trout can be seen on or near the surface. Confidence is key and I don't mind catching the odd out of season trout, if you're getting bites you feel more confident and fish better. Generally, I'm looking for a stretch of river that flows at a walking pace and not with lots of obstructions on the bottom looking for the odd boil on the surface as this gives away an obstruction on the river bed. It might be a lump of wood a change of depth or a weedbed, fish find these places great as they can hide from predators. What I don't want is a swim full of these type of obstructions as it makes it difficult to get a good trot down and I believe the fish will be split over a larger area. One or two obstructions concentrate fish the same goes for differences in flow any change from the average stretch of river needs to be investigated. Not all areas throw up fish but all changes in the river are worth a go.

Tactics for me are really simple and the theme remains the same regardless of species or seasons. I always prefer if I can to float fish for grayling. There's nothing better than watching that float disappear and the satisfying resistance felt when you strike. So, tackle needs to be balanced and light hours spent holding a rod and having to reel in every minute or so means there's no place for heavy rods and reels.

A visit to any match orientated tackle shop will have a selection of good float rods from twelve to seventeen feet to suit most pockets. I've a Garbolino twelve foot rod I use for small water fishing that cost less than forty pounds all the way up to a fifteen foot Drennan Acolyte that cost the best part of two hundred quid, although lately I find myself using a standard thirteen foot match rod as its probably the middle of the road length for small and larger venues. There's no need to again spend a fortune on reels, something in the two or three thousand size is fine and for thirty quid or so you can get a reel that a few years ago would have cost three times that much. A good floating line is needed to keep the line on the surface making it easier to lift off the water and set the hook, I prefer Drennan float fish it's been around for years so it stood the test of time any line that looks polished will work as I've always found these to be best for floating. Some anglers use some sort of floatant above their floats be it Vaseline or fly anglers floatant but I've never personally found it needed. Due to the nature of the different swims I find myself fishing, no one float is ideal so I find you have to use one that's ok for all swims. The nature of the roving grayling angler means you don't want to be tackling up every fifteen minutes. Roving allows you to cover more swims and also keeps the cold at bay.

I use Drennan crystal loafers in a variety of sizes as they are perfect in shallow swims and due to the dumpy nature of the float they carry a good amount of shot for their size meaning you control the float not the current, it also means you have enough weight to fish the odd deeper swim you might come across. I sacrifice a bit of stability in the deeper swims for the all-round use of the loafer in other areas.

The loafers are ideal also if the fishing is a little slow and you need to slow the float down to give the fish longer to take the bait as its bulbous tip means you can fish slightly overdept and drag a bit of line across the bottom without the float pulling under that will happen using a delicately shotted stick float.

Mainline is normally about four pounds to a hook link of something around two or three pounds to an eighteen or sixteen hook carrying double red or a red and a white maggot. If I can I always prefer a three pound hook link for two main reasons the first is I don't want to lose the fish of a lifetime and secondly grayling and trout can be found in the same areas and the small sandpaper teeth of the trout can lead to getting bitten off during the fight and nobody wants to leave a hook behind no matter how quickly the fish get rid of them. Shotting again is simple either a bulk of shot two thirds of the way down the line to one or two smaller droppers or what I've done recently is use the Drennan lock and slide olivetts using these allows me to alter my bulk either closer or further from my hook by simply sliding up the line without the risk of having to slide big shot up or down that can weaken it. A short six inch hook link allows you to fish that shallowest of swims with ease and that's all there is to it.

I've never spent too much time plumbing the swim I much prefer to choose my line to fish and trot through with a bare hook altering the depth till I drag bottom then I take half an inch of depth off. This is obviously just a starting point as I alter my depth again if I'm not getting bites either by shallowing up or more often than not adding depth and slowing the float down. Most of my bigger fish have come within the first half a dozen runs through either with minimal or no loose feed I find too much loose feed attracts the trout that can spoil your swim by leaping out the water or twisting and turning alerting ever other fish to the danger, indeed my biggest fish, a two pound fourteen ounce fish came first cast in a swim I'd not plumbed up in just had three or four runs through to gage the depth.

Just remember set your own targets and don't get hung up looking at pictures of great big fish some rivers grayling are scarce so any fish is an achievement others a pound is a big fish don't set yourself unrealistic targets you will soon lose the drive needed to catch it angling should be fun and bring the child out in all of us.

Autumn Memories

Darren Davies

Autumn is a season that creeps into our fading year, the landscape slowly donning the vivid reds and browns it is synonymous for. Although the temperatures are dropping, the leaves are reluctant to fall yet, only the brutal winds can persuade them otherwise, then they pirouette to the ground creating a beautiful mosaic, like a force 9 hitting an artist's palette, sweeping vibrant colours across the canvas.

Autumn has a pleasant aroma, many people try to replicate this by lighting candles that fragrant the home such as pumpkin, apple and pine.

As an all-round angler my thoughts, start to turn to barbel, zander and perch, boasting plump bellies as these fish harvest on what remains of the natural food and the small fry. Carp anglers realise that harder times are ahead and often look for a big hit this time of year, taking advantage of the carp's natural instinct to feed up before any possible big freeze.

Autumn sessions can often prove tricky, with the fish moving between their summer and winter haunts they are not always easy to locate.

Autumn brings the Harvest, succulent apples adorn the orchards, fungi burst through the leaf strewn fields and blooms of berries provide the resident birds a chance to feast, before the winter visitors, such as the Red-wing and Fieldfare arrive and gorge themselves after their long flight.

Even the anglers float, topped in dazzling orange feels more seasonal amongst the golden leaves on the water's surface as it sails through his hopeful swim, the angler ever encouraging the float to dip and result in a potbellied chub. Even the fish we catch are cloaked in vibrant colours this time of year, carp boast deep oranges and rusty browns, the tails of perch garnished in striking reds and barbel embellished in golden attire. With the ever changing weather this time of year, just like Bonfire night, autumn sessions can bring the angler fireworks on those red letter days where the fish get their heads down and you've located your quarry or they can leave you feeling haunted by the ghouls of Halloween, where the conditions seem ideal however the fish had other ideas. As some less fortunate animals will find out over the coming months, it can be feast or famine.

When it comes to barbel, during the hazy days of summer, my approach is a fun affair, they are out of condition after spawning and often can only be found in the faster shallower water, it's a tactic I enjoy however it's not until into autumn do I target them with the intention of landing the bigger specimens, as they start to move into the deeper water, usually after the first cold nights and shorter days set in. This time of year, my fishing is centred around evenings and early morning sessions, very often the sunrises and sunsets are masterpieces of subtle pinks and heart-warming oranges.

Perch can often be seen oppressing the smaller fish and fry into slacker areas of the river, such as marinas or dead arms as they methodically work as a group to inflict deadly strikes, temporarily stunning the fearful silvers into submission only to be engulfed as the perch opens its cavernous mouth leaving its prey no chance of escape.

On one of these red-letter days, I managed over 40 perch, 20 of which were over 2lb, the action, lasted less than a couple of hours, it was frantic and whichever lure I threw at them, they would hit with gusto. It seemed it would never end, however, all of a sudden, it was as if the marina was completely devoid of fish. Such is the importance of being in the right place at the right time in this bountiful season, it is very much a case of feast or famine. On stillwater's, the same can be seen in bays and around jetty's, if you spot fry leaping clear of the water, without hesitation cast your lure into that area, guaranteed, there will be predators very close by.

October 1st is the date that most predator anglers start their campaigns for pike, however for me, there is another predator that I prefer to target and that's the zander. Due to the zander being notoriously more difficult to catch in the depths of winter, I like to get a few under my belt earlier in the season when they are more active and will readily take a lure. Although the vast majority of my zander have been caught on the lure, which is a great way to catch them, especially as you stay mobile and cover lots of ground, this year I will target them using deadbaits a lot more, in the hope of landing the bigger specimens. The zander is a beautiful proud fish sporting bold stripes, translucent fins, vampire like teeth accompanied with large eyes, they are perfectly suited to hunting in low light conditions and for this reason, dusk is probably my favourite time to fish for them. This is when lures with vibration and an erratic action often work however, I have also had success with soft rubber shads.

Very often when fishing for zander in early autumn, pike will make a welcome appearance and are great sport this time of year, often tail walking their way out of trouble if the net doesn't find them first.
The bucolic surroundings are a pleasant environment for the angler and sometimes I wish the season could be longer, however, I suppose with the increase of milder winters, some years it does feel that autumn extends beyond its traditional 3 month period and can often feel like 4 or even 5 months before any sustained bitter conditions stop us in our tracks, which sees only the hardiest of anglers, often with ruddy faces, grace the banks. These "extended" autumns are where the carp angler can take advantage, with the carp being more active, there always feels like a good chance of a fish.

Feeding fish means catchable fish. This time of year, I use a boilie only approach as I believe the carp actively seek them out as their natural larder decreases and wanting to increase in weight for the winter, need to feed more often. However, if the weather in autumn does turn for the worse and the easterly winds take over, do not despair, natural baits, as in early spring, will often still catch you your quarry.

Last autumn, one session saw me land a couple of carp in a short period, fishing over a large bed of boilies, the day was mild and the night barely into single figures and my hunch was the carp would be feeding and they certainly obliged.

I will often fish a balanced bait this time of year, in the form of a snowman presentation or if the leaf litter is particularly bad a popped up bait on a multi-rig. As the weed and lilies die back, they still offer the carp protection, warmth and what is left of the natural food and these fish came to a bait fished near such a feature.

Autumn means something different to all anglers, for some, it's the start of something, for others it signals the end of something, to many, it provokes beautiful landscapes where pheasant calls echo through the woods, where the stags are rutting and nature out does itself each year with colours adorning every inch of the land, albeit only for a short period, however, it means the shorter days can be enjoyed even in adversity during those difficult sessions where the fish seem absent. Crunching leaves under foot, soon fade into the first hoarfrosts, as the angler leaves nothing but footprints on his early morning stroll along the river bank to his chosen swim. Get out and enjoy autumn, it may be over before you know it.

Things That Go Bump in the Night

Dave Mutton

If I was to say that they lurk in the darkness, some have spikes, some have sharp teeth others even have both you might wonder what I'm talking about. No, of course it isn't ghosts, ghouls and monsters, I'm talking about predators - namely pike, perch and zander. Primarily I want to talk about lure fishing for these fish, but I will probably digress at times and talk about bait fishing as well, so if you're not a plastic junkie with a rubber fetish don't worry, there is still hopefully something of interest in this piece for you. In fact, hopefully some of my observations are equally applicable if you are a worm botherer or deadbait drowner. Anyway, back to the point, I want you to imagine a scene, and if it helps you can substitute the word lure for worm!

An angler makes his way along the bank throwing lures in to likely looking spots as the light start to fade, the temperature starts to drop as the sun sinks below the horizon, he has 'one last cast' a few times and then makes his way back to his car, to drive back to the warmth and comfort of home. I'm sure this is a scenario that is familiar to all of you, but how about 'An angler makes his way along the bank, finding the spot with the help of his head torch, he quickly flicks out a jig into the inky black water, the first cast of many over the next few hours'? I bet this is a scenario that is a lot less familiar to many readers.

Lure fishing at night is something that I have done for a few years and I enjoy it immensely. When I talk about lure fishing at night, I am not talking about the height of summer as I'm targeting other species then, I mean through the autumn, winter and early spring months.

So why lure fish at night? Well, the reason is simply because it works, and works well. We often talk about 'the witching hour', that golden hour when all of a sudden, we start to get hits when previously the water seemed devoid of fish. Predators love low light levels as it makes them harder to spot as they lie in wait or glide through the gloom in search of a meal. Perch, zander and pike all have good eyesight so they can take advantage of the low levels to hunt prey without the prey being able to spot them so easily. However, in winter particularly, these low light conditions are very short-lived affairs, it goes from daylight to pitch black in about an hour or even less. So, if predators were to hunt as the sun started dropping and then stopped when it got dark, they would have a very short window of opportunity to find enough food to thrive and grow, or possibly even just to maintain weight. No, something I found out a few years back is that they will continue to feed right in to dark and sometimes for several hours after dark, even pike and perch.

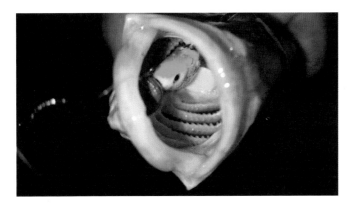

Zander anglers are well aware of the often nocturnal feeding habits of their target species and fish well into, and sometimes right through the night for them, traditionally using live or deadbaits so why not lures? They pick up on livies at night and they can and do see and feel lures moving through the water and will take them readily. It is the same with perch, often I have found that in the height of day the perch can be tucked away under boats, bushes and any other cover they can find and this can make it problematical fishing with lures.

We cast to the cover and then the first thing we do is reel the lure away from it – not very clever if we know that's where they are hiding out. Ok it could be argued that you can use a dropshot to try and keep a lure in position a lot longer than with say a jig head, and this is true but you are still positioning a bait on the outskirts of their territory and hoping to draw one out. This is the same when fishing with baits, you cast next to the boat not right under it. So how do you get right in to their territory with a lure at night? Let's face it, sometimes we seem to spend half our time casting in to bushes, getting hooked on boats etc in the middle of the day, so doing it at night would be a nightmare and cost a fortune (although that could be good for my lure sales!) luckily, we don't need to. I have found that as the light drops and fades in to darkness the perch will leave the sanctuary of cover and actively hunt in the open water. Good news as, on a canal for example, it's a damn site easier to cast one down the track than it is to flick it within an inch of the moored up canal barge!

Moving on to pike, for many years there was this perception that pike only feed during the day – wrong! Pike are far more active at night than a lot of people realise. Anybody that night fishes for zander, eels or catfish will confirm that as I'm betting most will have hooked a few pike depending on bait of course. It can be very useful to know this especially on crowded, pressured waters such as park lakes for examples. Often these contain pike which can be very tricky to catch.

In the day the park is full of joggers, dog walkers, cyclists, noisy kids etc and so the fish often back off and off until they are out of fishing range, certainly lure range anyway. As the light drops though this all changes, as the park gets quieter and quieter the pike will drift back to the near bank where they can be caught on lure or bait. Think about it, an angler packs up deadbaiting for the day, he has a couple of sardines, mackerel etc left, which, by this time are starting to look a bit sorry for themselves and so he throws them in to the water. He doesn't hurl them 60yards or more, they tend to land a few feet in to the margins, now the pike know this, they aren't stupid so you can guarantee that this is where they will be at the end of the day. So, it is well worth flicking a lure rod out after dark on this sort of venue, or if I was fishing baits, I would always have one rod right in the margins at night. One thing I will mention right now is please do not target pike at night, particularly on baits, unless you are an already competent pike angler. We will discuss this in more detail later on but everything will be that bit harder to do in the dark so you don't want to be unhooking a fish with 700 teeth unless you know exactly what you are doing, safety is paramount, both yours and the pikes.

So, apart from the gear you would need for lure fishing generally, what else do you need? Well, the most obvious thing is a head torch, without one your session will be a nightmare and possibly very short lived. The right clothing is vital, once that sun goes down the temperatures can plummet in the winter so good thermal clothing that is going to keep you dry is a must along with good walking boots. A buff, hat and possibly some gloves as you will really feel the dip in temperatures on exposed areas of skin. I quite often take a flask of coffee with me as well. I may not actually take it fishing, but I can always return to the van and grab a coffee and warm up a bit if it gets too cold. The other thing I always carry with me through the winter months, especially at night, is a bottle of glycerine. I have lost count of the times that I'm fishing away ok for the last couple of hours of light, then it gets dark, the temps dip and I start to get that feeling that my reel isn't working properly and everything is a bit stiff and jerky- it isn't the reel at all, it is ice forming in the rings of your rod. A cotton bud, dipped in glycerine (available from chemists) and then rubbed around the ceramic inserts on your rod will sort this out. You may well have to re-apply several times during the session but it only takes a minute and it will keep you fishing.

Apart from the precautions from the cold, and being able to see, what else do you need to think about? Well it is important to realise that everything will seem that much more difficult at night. For example, if you are a bit short sighted, then threading flouro through a jig head can be difficult and frustrating, so it might be worth considering making some pre tied rigs up at home and winding them on to a rig bin like pike and carp anglers use. At least then you will only then have to tie a fresh leader to your braid. Know the area you will be fishing. You will have limited visibility, so at night is probably not the best time to be exploring new water, fish to the tried and tested, you may be pleasantly surprised at how much better they feed at night too. Do not fish areas that are difficult to access during the day as they will be a lot harder to access during the night.

So, what lures do you need and how do you fish them? I suppose the obvious choice would be small rattling crankbaits, funnily enough I use these very seldom on the river as they are definite pike magnets. Now I love lure fishing for pike, but generally I am targeting perch. It isn't that the pike won't feed at night, they do and I regularly catch them when perch fishing, but I find that the pike are often more obliging during the day than the perch so will target them during the day. So, most of my fishing is on soft rubber lures. I am generally looking for something that I can work fairly slowly but will displace a fair amount of water and has good tail movement at slow speed. Some of my current favourites are the Gunki Grubby Shad, Wake Flexfish and K.P Baits Skeleton Shad. I don't bother with ultra small baits and wasping techniques at night, the smallest I go is a 2" lure but even then, I'm looking for something fairly substantial and they must certainly have a good paddle on them. As the temperature and the colour starts to drop out of the river my approach usually shifts to deadsticking, now this takes a leap of faith, fishing a lure that is essentially stationary at night, but, trust me, it works! My Lure of choice for this is the Z-Man Pogyz. I have caught so many perch on this lure I prefer to use floating lures for deadsticking so the Z-Man products suit perfectly. Gunki have just introduced a floating version of the Grubby Shad too so I am looking at putting that through its paces. The original Grubby Shad has been a fantastic lure for me in the 6 months or so that I have been using it and has already given me perch to 3.8lb and a pike which I measured at 105cm. I also fish the Ned rig at night as it is a natural progression from deadsticking and can be fished stationary. Obviously, Z-Man baits such as the Finesse TRD and Finesse shad along with TRD craws etc work well here. One thing I have started doing ever increasingly is fishing Ned rigs using a worm or wide gape hook on a Cheburashka weight. This gives a bit more flexibility and wobble to a bait which often induces takes at night. Also, the shroomz heads seem to rust very quickly so I don't tend to use these so much these days. A new lure which I have only just received and I am really excited about using is the new SWD Swimming

Dragonfly from Molix. This is a floating lure shaped like a dragonfly larvae with lots of wriggly fluttering short legs and a ribbed body. I haven't had a chance to use it yet but it looks really good.

So, what colour lure? Basically, whatever you have in your box! I have caught on everything from pearl through to black. Far more important than colour is the action of the lure and how much it 'rings the dinner bell'. There are a multitude of soft plastics with glow in the dark variants and I do use these but only if the lure itself is right, this is far more important to me than if it glows or not. There are also many scented lures available on the market and these possibly give more of an edge than glow in the dark colours as, in my opinion, when perch are hunting at night, they are not just relying on sight to find prey but are picking up on vibration and scent. I will say that if you are fishing areas where a lot of light falls on the water, boat moorings etc then dark lures fished up in the water can do brilliantly well as they silhouette really nicely. Zander will often hide on the edges of lit areas waiting for prey, which are often attracted to the light, and strike from out of the darkness. I would also say learn to know your lures. I very rarely fish new lures at night as it is easier to really test them and familiarise yourself with the lure in the day, once I am confident that I can get the best out of the lure then I will start using it at night.

So far, I have talked about the cold, reduced visibility, difficulties, so why on earth would you want to do it? You will soon find out why when you give it a go and get a big perch or zander slam your lure out of nowhere in the dark, one of those hits that you feel right through the back of your hand. When you are bringing a moderate perch back to the waiting net, turn on your head torch and see a great fat perch following it in or a huge shape like a missile lurking in the margins. When you are fishing for zander, feel a solid thump in the dark and feel that stubborn shaking on the line, you bring the fish up, turn on the head torch and see a great big pink eye gleaming back at you out of the darkness. You will enjoy having the bank to yourself and targeting fish that don't give themselves up readily during the day.

Hopefully this article has given food for thought for you. All I can say is give it a go, it may put a few extra fish on the bank for you and you may enjoy it, I have to say I love fishing for things that go bump in the night.

My Way with Barbel

Jerry Gleeson

My preparations for a new season start before the old one has even ended, come march sometimes earlier I will start thinking about new waters I'd like to fish or new stretches in the coming season, hours will be spent on google earth, what a fabulous tool this is for checking out new stretches of river especially if you're like me and can't drive, local train stations will be found and routes will be plotted, swims can be found and you can get a good feel for the river without actually setting foot on it.

I must spend a small fortune on trains and taxis so I also spend lots of time scrolling through ticket operators to find out when it's cheaper to travel, essential if you're like me and will jump on a train at the drop of a hat, sometimes though it's not always the case I've had many trips with my good pals Matt Marlow, Paul Floyd, Rich Parsons, Julian Barnes and many others and we've had some great adventures along the way.

From May onwards I spend lots of time on my local river, the Goyt, not only is it a fantastic time to be by the river as everything is coming back to life the fish are so much easier to tempt onto the shallows, I've spent hours up on hours fish spotting at this time of the year. Being a spate river, it can change so much from one season to the next, in years gone by I've mapped the river bed out with a fish finder, these days I'm content with the old fashioned way of leading about.

Pellets and boilies will be fed to ravenous chub and when we're lucky the occasional barbel will come right in, again hours, days infact have been spent watching how fish react to bait and to how bait behaves in the water.

When they're not water damaged (there's a nasty rumour going round that I've dropped the occasional camera in) I will take picture after picture of swims, as tree's spring to life and the water levels rise and fall this can pay dividends in knowing where close in snags and drop offs are, come a bit of high water your catching fish where you would normally sit at low level. Time spent learning your own river is time well spent as this can be taken onto new venues.

Summer/Autumn

A lot of my barbel fishing whether on a small, medium or large river is based around using lots of small particle baits, hemp seed, pigeon conditioner, micro pellets all heavily glugged to break down and give off loads of scent, my favourite hook bait is a dumbbell usually 14mm which if need be can be broken in half and hair rigged.

A bait dropper is a major part of my armoury, whether your baiting a tight area or spreading your bait over a larger area, there's nothing more accurate than a dropper, there's all different shapes and sizes and from every manufacturer, personally I prefer the small and medium Seymo ones.

When targeting smaller rivers and once we've chosen our swim I'll always start by introducing between 10 and 20 small droppers of hemp and micro pellets then one or 2 droppers of broken boilies and dumbbells. The swim will be left to rest for up to an hour, before making my first cast I introduce 5 more, if we're lucky and the barbel move in straight away they can devour 20 droppers of tiny particles in no time at all, the 5 droppers will hopefully bring them back in, should the barbel not move in straight away we have minnows, roach, dace and the ever hungry chub to deal with so we're topping up the swim to add more attraction.

I much prefer to use leads than feeders on smaller rivers and these will incorporate a PVA bag of micro pellets and broken boilies, there's no rule as to how often ill recast, if the tips remain motionless I'll go in with the dropper again, if there's plenty of activity I can cast as often as 15 minutes, other times I'll leave it an hour, it generally all depends on the barbel population and the silver population, on the Goyt there's hardly any small silvers, just annoying chub, on the Derwent there's millions of dace and chublets that will be smashing your baits to bits so I will cast a bit more often, once it goes dark and the silvers disappear ill regularly recast every hour.

As I travel to most places on the train the majority of my fishing is done from 5pm to 9am, pretty much peak barbel feeding times, as a rule I don't rove about, generally because I have too much gear and I've been travelling all day, I do much prefer to work at a swim, if after a few hours we've caught nothing or had no indications, I will move and start the process again, if I'm unlucky I occasionally have to do it a third time.

Rigs are pretty straight forward certainly nothing technical, I always use a running rig, Korum do a good running rig or there's the lone angler running rings, hook link is straight forward size 8 swivel, anti-tangle tubing to prevent tangle on the cast and these days I much prefer using long hook links of braid or fluorocarbon from 3-5ft, as for the hair rig this is usually about half a centremetre from hook, from personal experience I've found if I have the bait tight to the hook, I hook a lot of chub and the same if I use a long hair of 2 inch, in fact I've had some of my most vicious chub takes on long hairs, I find having the hair about a centremetre away keeps the chub at bay and often results in mainly snatches, others may have different experience's but these are mine and it works for me.

On the bigger rivers I fish, well there's only one really, I do flirt with the

Ribble occasionally and the Wye but a river like the Trent, well that's a beast all on its own although the Wye is a big river it's not a patch on the Trent especially the tidal. It's not really my type of fishing, bivvy's, bedchairs, alarms and tripods coupled with big heavy feeders or leads, the tidal Trent itself is daunting and barren and the style of fishing alien to most. I refuse to buy a bivvy, I like to sit by my rods, I've bought an over wrap for my storm shelter that's as far as I'm going, admittedly in the depths of winter on the tidal you do need some comfort.

Back to the baiting, exactly the same as the smaller rivers only a lot more, I will bait up a good area and fish a feeder on top of the baited area and recast every 10-15 minutes, down the back of the swim I'll fish a straight lead with a single bait. There are masses of silver fish in the Trent so I find it important to keep the bait going in, my only worry with fishing loads of particles is the bream, not usually a massive problem in the day but at night they can be a pain, usually a larger hook bait keeps them at bay.

Certain parts of the Trent for whatever reason I can't buy a bite on boilies or pellets in the day same as the beach area on Sutton around the little bush, maybe it's just me or maybe it's because these areas get hammered more than others and the fish are more wary, in cases like this I switch to the humble maggot, the maggot feeder and very long hook links up to 8 feet a very alien way of catching barbel to me until I started fishing the Trent and a very deadly method.

With a stretch of river like the tidal Trent where there are no visible features it will pay dividends to lead about and find them, if you're lucky enough to own one use a fish finder to map out the bottom to find the features and drop offs. In the summer time especially when the rivers are low and clear whether your fishing a small or big river it's important to know your surroundings, as I said earlier take as many pictures as possible, get your polaroid's on, get your fish finder out or lead about, get your homework done now this will come to fruition come the winter months.

Late Autumn/Winter

Come late autumn early winter the weather becomes a bit erratic, so does my baiting approach, from frosty nights and bright sunny cold days to warm overcast rainy days and nights and occasionally periods of snow, 1 week is always different from the next. Unlike summer and autumn where the fish are very active and will feed whenever they choose, the barbel have now moved to their winter homes and will only feed as and when, sometimes on my local river it's been possible to time your watch by a bite, the colder it is the less they feed but they still feed, from our homework in the summer we know where they live, the key is tempting them to feed or at least being on the bank when they do.

My baiting approach depends on the weather, sudden temperature drops on a low clear river will see me stay at home, once the temperature has stabilised and the fish have acclimatised I will be back on the river, I will still use particles but I rely heavily on heavy scented baits from big meat to boilies I've had glugged for months and lots of paste, in cold frosty weather generally I will use a feeder packed with paste so I have that constant scent in the water hookbait will consist of a matching dumbbell hookbait that I've had glugged for some time.

At some point after the cold spell we're going to get some horrible cold rain that will fill the rivers up, there's nothing worse, however as the river rises, the currents become stronger the fish have to move and if they're moving they're using energy which means they eventually have to feed, there's nothing worse than being sat on the river with a cold north easterly wind and rain, the vast majority of the time I'd rather stay home but if my working week or family time means this is my only chance to get out I will, my approach is simple big single smelly bait, my favourite being paste wrapped boilies. Swim choice I'm looking for a deep slack area or a slower deeper area with a drop off where the fish will be taking shelter.

I spend a lot of time in the winter watching the weather on various apps although I do fish in the most unfavourable weather and successfully catch (occasionally) I'd much rather fish in more favourable conditions, you can't beat some nice low pressure coupled with high day and night time temps and some lovely rain to warm up the rivers, when I can I'll even plan my working week round a good warm spell.

My approach again totally different to the last, when the waters warmed up there's extra water on and the fish have to move and like I said before if they move there using energy and they need to feed.

We're now back on the particles lots of micro pellets, ground bait and lots and lots of glug, this will be packed into a feeder and cast repeatedly at regular intervals, some will stay in the swim most will be washed down river and with it all that lovely scent that will get those barbules twitching, this kind of weather if you time it right its fill your boots time, well it should be if the barbel are behaving, but do they ever!

River Carp Fishing

Dale Thomas

I first found out about the Tidal Severn around Tewkesbury in 2015, off a good friend and excellent angler, John Mott, who used to fish it regularly. I met John while I was fishing the Trent. He pointed out that if I didn't mind a lot of blanks, the lower/tidal Severn was a lot closer than the Trent. A day ticket tidal stretch was suggested, so a plan was hatched. On my first visit I somehow managed to catch a stunning thick set barbel weighing 11lb 13oz.

The barbel were always going to be my main target but I had heard that carp were also being caught. I had fluked one mirror carp out of the Wye earlier in the season, so they were still fresh in my mind. As predicted, a few blank 24hr sessions followed, however I was catching a few nice pike and small zander in the day and never actually blanked.

During the next session I hit the jackpot over a big bed of hemp and boilies, landing my first tidal Severn carp. It came into the margin very easily but then proceeded to tear up and down the margins!! Eventually I stopped it doing this by sticking the net in front of it, a little under gunned using my Greys 1.5tc barbel rods, but it was in the net. The only fish of the session - a stunning carp and still my PB river mirror carp, weighing 22lb 5oz.

A few weeks went by before I could return. This gave me time to hatch a 'Catch a Carp' plan. With the tidal Severn being 50 miles away, pre-baiting wasn't an option, but fishing over a big bed of bait seemed to be the way to go. As I would be fishing for at least 48hrs, I soaked/cooked up 20kg of hemp. Unfortunately, this was before I started using Monster Particle, so it was hard work.   Also, a total of 6kg of 3FootTwitch mixed size/flavour boilies to be added to the bucket of spomb mix or fed on their own as needed. On arrival to the river, around 11am, the entire stretch was, as usual, deserted, despite it being a sunny August weekend. Perfect.

The spombing commenced with around 5-6kg being spread to a tree-lined far margin. This is where I had caught the previous barbel and carp. Accuracy wasn't really an issue as I wanted a big spread of bait covering a large area. Mixed into the particle was around 2kg of mixed boilies - more than I had ever used anywhere!! I set up the bivvy and other kit slowly, in no hurry to start fishing. Around 3pm I cast out the two carp rods on the baited area. These needed to have a back lead until the boat traffic stopped, around 7pm - one down the margin with a live-bait for zander or pike. I had a few small zander - one with some very big teeth marks in it from being attacked by a monster on the way in.

I set up the bivvy and other kit slowly, in no hurry to start fishing. Around 3pm I cast out the two carp rods on the baited area. These needed to have a back lead until the boat traffic stopped, around 7pm - one down the margin with a live-bait for zander or pike. I had a few small zander - one with some very big teeth marks in it from being attacked by a monster on the way in.

As dusk approached, I reeled in the zander rod to relax and concentrate on the carp rods. After recasting with 2x16mm boilies on each rod, plus a long 6-8 boilie PVA stringer, I put the kettle on and sat outside the bivvy with a brew. Using both alarms and rod tip lights means I don't have to sit with eyes glued to rod tips all night, plus a receiver means I can get some kip without reeling in. Just alarms would be enough, but it's great to see what the tips are doing when you get a few beeps or a run.

The first fish of the night was an unmistakable screamer of a run, hard-fighting but very much easier to control using 2.75tc Fox Warrior carp rods. Soon in the net after a few hard runs up the margin was a pale mirror carp weighing 12lb 9oz. A great start.

Only 40 mins later the same rod was off again, another pale mirror carp, almost identical to the last one and, at 10lb 11oz. another double. They were obviously here on the feed, so I spombed in another half a bucket of particle/boilies into the darkness. It was at this point I noticed the tide had reached this part of the river, up around three foot and slowing up. Both rods were recast to the sand spots. An hour or two went past before the next fish and river carp number three. Yet another pale fish that must have escaped from the same lake during a flood. At 9lb 15oz it was just short of a double. No more bait was added, I simply recast with stringer attached.

Just before dawn another screaming take resulted in the fourth and last fish of the first night - another mirror carp weighing 10lb 11oz. It would soon be boat traffic time, so I reeled in for some much-needed rest, not planning on waking until dinner time at the earliest. It can often be difficult fishing the tidal Severn in daylight hours, boat traffic ranges from small barges to ocean going yachts! Autumn/winter, when Tewkesbury lock is shut, things are a lot quieter, but this was summer-time and the boats were constant. I rebaited with most of the last bucket of particle/boilies around 4pm, then had something to eat and a coffee before casting to the baited area just before dusk. A couple of hours passed by..... just long enough for a few doubts to set in. After all, I had caught four carp the previous night. Was it expecting too much to catch more carp tonight?

Fortunately, shortly after I had another alarm bursting screamer of a run. I could feel the line pinging off the far bank tree line! Once mid-river it was an easier fight to win. My first tidal Severn common carp was in the net, weighing 13lb 10oz. The rest of my remaining bait was spombed out - 1kg boilies, 5kg of hemp. Only half an hour later and I was into another fish. Weighing in at 11lb 8oz, a really pretty mirror carp.

Settling down in the bivvy after a celebratory coffee, I was woken by a screaming alarm again just before dawn. The final fish was a second common weighing 9lb 14oz. That ended my first – and, to date, my best - tidal Severn carp session, which, brought seven carp between 9lb and 13lb over two nights.

Chevin Chaser

Vito Napoli

For a while I've not been able to get around as much as I'd like to. Having been involved in a car crash had set me back both mentally and physically for the best part of 20 months. Not being that mobile really limited where and when I could fish and my usual roving sessions were out of the question. Thankfully I'm on the mend and fishing has really helped me get through the turmoil. Having snowballed in my plans, I can now start writing a few articles for this great online magazine and a few others, so watch this space.

I know most anglers prefer to target chub during the winter months, it's understandable because it's when they are most active; scavenging for food and thus putting on the pounds and ounces, but I enjoy stalking them during the summer months just as much as the winter. Chub are my all time favourite species, the Houdini of fish, the only species capable of taking your hook bait without any notification on your rod tip, they are masters at putting you into the deepest snags, and they will most certainly take you to the cleaners, quickly, if you don't bully them enough from the second you feel that first head bang. They are powerhouses, full of muscle, built like Irish show bulls! And the Gt Ouse chub are not about length, but girth! I love our chub down south, mainly short in the body but full of girth, just how a chub should look like in my books.

I'll be absolutely honest with you, my tactics, baits and rigs do not change. I always use a very simple running rig, and I don't like my line to be too busy, the less I have on the line the better. I use the least amount of shot to hold bottom, this could be just a BB shot, but I don't fish lightly, you have to tend with serious snags, and of course a thicker line helps you play in and around the weed beds during the summer months. I like my shot at least 4 to 5ft away from the hook. At the point of connecting with the fish, I allow a bow of line out, letting the shot/lead do the work before I commit myself. Also, I use a thicker line because there's a good chance of hooking into a barbel. Don't believe what people say 'There are no barbel in the Ouse anymore' Well I can assure you there are, but they are not easy to catch. Since September I've caught 18 whilst fishing for chub, with the smallest weighing 7lb 10oz and the largest 13lb 1oz. Therefore, I use lines no less than 10lbs straight through to hooks ranging from size 8 to 2. I use Korda wide gape micro barbed, they remain nice and sharp and hold onto the fish very well.

I only use natural baits and I offer large pieces straight on the hook. Bread, cheese, meat, lobworms and slugs, and on those baits, I have caught 100's of good size chub. You can easily get caught up in using all different kinds of attractants and flavourings, I don't use them. Then there's the cheese paste wars, I'm not going to get into that either, and again I never make or use cheese paste. A good strong mature cheddar is just as good, and I've found an excellent way of nipping a piece onto the hook that allows it to break free on the strike. Those that know me will vouch for this method that I use time and time again. That said, all the other baits that I've mentioned and choose not to use do have proven track records. The most important factor when it comes to bait, is making sure it behaves naturally in the water.

My rods are mainly split cane. Something you don't see or hear about these days, maybe too outdated for the modern day angler, AKA the garden bean pole! I use a Chapmans 500 (Avon style) that has a luscious action and balance, and WA Allcocks Adonis (Bottom rod) with a Sealy Twin Taper top. Great powerful rod with a lovely sensitive tip to detect the slightest pluck from any wily chub. Both have high millage with a lot of adventures under their belts.

Most recently I was testing a prototype split cane rod (Mk1 Chevin Chaser) which was made and gifted to me by an Instagram follower and rod makers, Achim Bandszus and Markus Leo, who own Colliery Cane Rods based in Germany. This particular rod was made from old tonkin bamboo with plenty of strong power fibres. Although I prefer 10ft rods, due to choosing tight swims and narrow stretches, this is 11ft, two piece, plus a detachable handle of 28 inches. The whippings are gorgeous with Gudebrod nylon in medium brown. The ferrules are made from bronze and the rings are traditional high bell. It has a hollow build mid-section, and the top being solid. The blank was tempered in a heater for 35 mins at 170°c!

The day I received it from Germany, I primed the rod and hit the river. That evening I had a scrap with 9lb 12oz barbel, and this rod performed superbly, it has a beautiful action. To date, using this rod I have landed three barbel into double figures and many 5lb plus chub. My Acolyte 14ft float and 10ft feeder rods, which I must say are excellent rods when it comes to carbon, are sadly accumulating dust. I'm sure they will get a waggle before the end of the season. Split cane isn't everyone's cup of tea, some may laugh when they read this article, but I think I can justify how good they really are, and they give me all the confidence I need to catch chub and barbel with. There's good and bad in traditional rods as in carbon, but pick a good one that has lots of meat and they will perform superbly and last a very long time. They shouldn't be underestimated, and they really come alive when you lock onto a fish. I use mine daily, in all weathers, and they are extremely strong with lots of gears and backbone to help you control and bring in those powerful fighting river fish.

My reels are all Mitchell 300's, good old coffee grinders! They are such an iconic reel, very versatile and can take a hammering, and I do hammer them a lot. They have never let me down and all those years later, after rolling off the production line, I honestly believe they are still the best looking reels out there and ever so reliable. One of the reels I use a lot is 42 years old, the same age as me! They are easy to maintain and have a great front facing clutch on them. Timeless pieces of equipment.

I'm lucky that I live right on top of the Gt Ouse, and it's known for great quality chub, roach, barbel and oh yes, otters. I have bumped into them many a time when out fishing, and when others would move on, I've always remained in situ because I've still caught decent fish not long after they have disappeared. I'm not sticking up for them by any means, and they do need controlling, but they have never given me any issues when fishing and it appears the fish are not that bothered by them. Something to think about....

Being so close to lots of narrow winding stretches of the Ouse, it helps me keep a close eye on the river. You'll be surprised what you see and how much info you can gather by walking the banks. I do not trust phone apps that give you river levels, purely because they do not get updated enough, so the best method is to visit the stretch (if you're local) and see for yourself. That way you can make your own mind up whether you intend to fish or not. Plus, it gives you a chance to speak to other anglers and see how they are getting on. Knowledge goes a long way.

With all this recent flooding, many anglers choose not to fish. This could be for many reasons, and safety is paramount in these conditions. But if you are like me, I like to take advantage fishing in floods. Chub fishing in such conditions isn't easy, but if you can get in any slacks and eddies, tucking your bait right up against a feature then you have a good chance of hooking into a decent chevin. Chub will stay tight in those areas saving energy and will wait for any food to come their way. Smelly baits in coloured water is best and I will never move off to another swim for at least 30 to 40 minutes. You have to give the fish time to smell your bait, then build the confidence up to take it. You may be lucky, it's happened to all of us, that you will get a take within seconds/minutes of your bait hitting the river bed. If not sit and wait, they will arrive if they are interested and hungry. I read too many posts on social media where people are advising anglers to move swims just merely after 10 to 15 minutes. It can take double that time to get a decent chub to gather its confidence. You'll be lifting that bait away from its nose, just as it was ready to nab your bait and a chance then lost. Just be patient and sit quietly. Once I cast in it stays there, I dislike working a swim, the less disturbance the better. Most of my bites come within 30 minutes, if nothing develops after that time I will move on.

I'm not going to talk about the best conditions to catch chub. I have caught both chub and barbel in all weathers, and chub in particular I have caught in the darkest chocolate coloured rising waters. My PB of 7lb 3oz chub was caught in a raging flood and the water was so rich in colour that I was expecting to see Augustus Gloop float past! I have broken all the rules that have been set in stone and have caught chub and barbel. They are wild animals and if they are hungry, they will feed in any conditions and at any time of the day or night. The only time I would not fish is in high winds. It's a personal thing, I just hate winds, it makes me feel very uncomfortable, but other than that I will be out there targeting chub.

Most of my chub are caught less than a rods length away. Fishing so close not only allows me to pin point my cast, next to or under a feature, but in my experience the bigger fish are closer in than you think. I touch ledger and watch the tip at the same time. So many chub have been caught by feeling movement, plucks in between my thumb and index finger. It's a great method to use and you rarely miss a bite. Fishing so close becomes a hit and hold situation, and my clutch is always on lock down, I do not want to give that chub a chance to snag me. Locking onto a decent 5 or 6lb chub will bolt like a bat out of hell to the nearest cover. I need to take that fish away from its comfort zone asap and call the shots. However, some you win, and some you lose. I take my hat off to every chub that sends me to the cleaners.

Like I said, my article isn't about how you should fish for chub and what methods and baits are best to use. Everyone has their own way of doing things, there's no right or wrong. I don't get involved nor have time for over opinionated people that think they know best, just fish the way you want, if you're catching on a certain method or bait then great, just enjoy fishing, your time at the water's edge, it's not a competition.

I have, in not too much detail, written what works for me and in return my methods have given me great results. As a member of the Chub Study Group we record all chub over 4lb in weight, and without burying my head into my records I cannot give you an accurate number of how many chub over 4, 5 and 6lb I've caught so far this season, but it's a wealthy number, I must be doing something right!

One chap asked me how I catch so many chub. "Do you just lob your bait in and wait, because I only catch chublets", I wish it was that easy. I have caught chub on the float, sight fishing and on the feeder, but there's a great challenge fishing from the tip. Your rod tip needs to be your best friend, you need to know how to read it inside and out to not miss the slightest bite. However, to catch specimen chub you really need to know what you're doing, where to cast, how long to leave your bait out, what baits to use and how to present those baits. Of course, there's an element of luck needed too and time, the list is quite endless, but the most important thing for me is knowing or getting to know the stretch of river you are fishing. That means spending quality time on the river bank, lots of walking and observing, and taking notes. Build up your knowledge, your watercraft skills, because it will definitely help you to choose those special swims. Let's not forget that certain swims will attract the bigger fish. I know a holding area where I've caught more than one chub, four in fact all being over 5lbs, other areas will produce low to mid 4's. I am always learning, I don't think you can ever stop learning on how to fish.

Chub will eat anything put in front of them, they are not line or hook shy, but they're also not stupid, far from it. If your bait presentation is presented in a willy nilly fashion then they will suss that out quickly, become suspicious and ignore it. Take time presenting your bait, have the right balance, choose your swims carefully, use all your watercraft skills, be very patient and be different, then you may outwit a decent chub or two.

A very recent 7lb 3oz pristine chevin caught using my Chapmans 500 split cane rod, paired with a Mitchell 300 reel. A morning session using a large piece of cheddar cheese, casted between two hawthorn bushes approximately 4ft away from the bank. A very memorable session and PB that will be hard to beat.

Red Hot Carpin'

Gareth Thomas

I thought I'd chat about my experience in the summer months. I've had some great sessions in the warmer months. I think it's perfect for a bit of surface fishing. You can't beat it when you're enticing the carp to the surface with some dog biscuits and eventually one falling for the trap and getting that bend in the rod. I've also had plenty of success just fishing small PVA bags of crushed boilie fished on the bottom.

I would like to talk about a session from July 2018. One of my mates posted to my group on Facebook that he was booking a peg for 48 hours on the Horseshoe lake at Cefn Mably and wondered if anyone would like to join him. I remember thinking at the time, I haven't been here for over a year as most of my time has been at The Birch since I joined. I immediately replied with a massive YES! I called the shop on site to confirm the booking and pay. The Horseshoe holds a decent head of carp with a few going over 20lb. The lake has 8 pegs with a gravel path to make it a lot easier to get to the pegs. The lake was originally constructed in 1993 and has matured lovely over the years. The fishery has done a lot of work reinforcing some pegs and making them spacious. They have even added some log cabins to make the fishing experience a lot better.

We had a scorching summer in 2018. It was so hot it made me a little nervous as I thought the carp would not be on the feed. We had it over 20 degrees for 4 weeks solid. Not even a drop of rain. You could visually see all the lakes had dropped a few feet on water level. I even rang ahead to see if it was still fishable as I was quite concerned with the oxygen levels. The fishery said it was, but to be honest I was still a little concerned. I checked the forecast and saw that we had a spell of rain coming in and was hoping this would come when I was fishing as it would switch them back on the feed after the influx of oxygen from the rain.

On the Friday I set off to the lake. I had to be there for 4pm. I left a little early, so I made a slight detour to KFC for a twister meal. It was bloody lovely too and set me up lovely for the night ahead. I arrived at the venue and checked in to get the code for the gate. I asked how it has been fishing and the chap said it's been quite hard. I remember thinking maybe we should have waited a few weeks for the weather to turn. But I said nope, I like a challenge.

Lenny was already setting up when I arrived. We had pegs three and four with me being on three. I always take my overwrap with me whether its summer or winter as It keeps me cooler in the summer and warmer in the winter. I've never fished this side of the lake before and was a little gutted when I got on the peg. It clearly wasn't big enough for me to use my overwrap. Also, the banks were a lot higher this end compared to the other end with respect of the lake losing a couple of feet with this weather we had. I managed to squeeze my 2-man bivvy on and put everything in place before casting out.

The lake bed was silty with no underlying weed, so I thought I would fish a simple knotless knot style rig with a little silicone on the shank of the hook to help the hook turn. Currently, I was using Northern Baits. I decided to use the Milky Amino on the one rig and a snow man rig with the same boilie but topped with the Kiwi Fruit Milky Amino pop up on the other. As always, I must put something on the end of the rig, whether it's a PVA bag with crushed boilie or some foam but for me it's a must each time no matter how close in your fishing. This time I decided on some crushed boilie in some PVA mesh hooked on. My swim had a perfect feature in it. Just to the left and the right was a cluster of lily pads. The left was a lot bigger than the right, but the plan was to fish right on the edge of each of the pads. You don't have to cast very hard on

The Horseshoe, just a gentle lob is perfect. That is exactly what I'd done. I firstly cast to the left of the pads, felt the lead down and started to settle my line. As I put the rod down to put the bobbin on, the line went tight. I couldn't believe my luck as I was told it wasn't fishing very well but within 1 minute I was bent into a fish. Even Lenny couldn't believe how lucky I was. It wasn't a massive fish, but it certainly put to bed my earlier worries about the weather making it difficult to get some fish on the bank.

After returning the prize back home I managed to get the two rods out on my chosen spots. This time I managed to settle the lines and attach the bobbins. I decided to catapult a few free offerings over each spot, thinking that if they are still in the area this may keep them there. Right on que the same rod ripped off again. I genuinely couldn't believe my luck. This lake has been fishing quite hard due to the scorching weather we had and there's me having two takes within the first thirty minutes. To this day I still get that buzz when you see the gorgeous bar of gold coming over the net cord and this one was no different. This was a little bigger than the last one but again not the biggest.

The rest of the day just got better and better. Lenny had a couple on the bank and I started to lose count on how many I had. We had a bit of a social up on Lenny's swim with my receiver turned up. The good thing about this lake is the swims are close enough to have a social with your mates. The rods stayed quiet for a few hours which was good as we managed to have a good chat and listen to all the other bite alarms roar off on the other lakes. It gave us a well-earned rest.

The night turned into a sleepless one for me. The alarms never stopped, and the weather took a turn for the worse. It absolutely hammered down which obviously switched the carp back on. It got to the point that I was catching so many we decided only to take photos of the better-looking ones. All the takes were on the left rod so that was on the sweet spot. I thought I would change the right rod from the Milky Amino to the BNB to see if that would spring that rod to life. Not that I needed to catch anymore, especially in this weather. The plan worked within an hour; the right rod came to life. A pattern began to form with at least one of the rods going off every hour. It was about 3am and I was wrecked. I made the choice to reel in as I needed some well-earned rest. But I made sure I baited the spots to keep them feeding while there were no lines in the water. Finally, some rest!

The rain continued through the night but eased off about 7am. I managed to get the rods back out while it stopped raining, with Lenny having the same idea. I asked how his night was thinking it would have been the same as mine. I was shocked when he said he didn't have one bleep. I explained how restless my night was while showing him the photos I took. He agreed that some were lovely looking. Again, the fish were not the biggest, but it was fun and that's what it's all about. The rest of the session was prolific. Lenny managed a few more which was nice to see. I even managed to film him playing one. A good bit of footage for my YouTube channel. I won't keep writing about each catch as it was so many for the both of us. But in all, it was an awesome session that I will always remember. Yes, the fish were not the biggest but it's not all about catching big fish all the time. Sometimes it's nice just to get away and have a bit of fun. This was the first time I met Lenny and we both enjoyed it thoroughly. And that's what fishing is all about. You get to meet so many good people on the bank who you can share memories with. This is also what we wanted to achieve with my Facebook group. We wanted to achieve something a bit different with the group. We didn't want it to be just a like and share group. We wanted to interact with the members.

We went on to organise a charity match at White Springs Fishery in September. Lenny fished the match as well, but he contributed a lot to the match. He managed to organise some fantastic donations for the raffle prizes we had. The match was a great turnout. We had twenty-two anglers who fished. This was the first time I have ever organised something like this and I was hoping it would run smoothly. I wasn't let down either. It couldn't have gone any better. Everyone played a major role in making this charity match and I would like to say a huge Thank You to everyone who took part. We had set a target for £100 and we hit that and raised £1007. The charity we raised this for was The Anthony Nolan Blood Cancer.

As this was a huge success, we have decided to organise another charity match. This one is for The Stroke Association. This is booked at Willow Park Fishery at the end of February 2020. The Stroke Association was chosen by Lenny as this is close to his heart. I wanted to do it for his choice of charity as a way of saying Thanks for all his hard work on the first charity match. Not that no one else contributed but he went above and beyond. I'm grateful for all the hard work he done for the cause and without that help I don't think we would have raised so much. So, Thank You.

Targeting Big Barbel & Chub

Brett Longthorne

I first started barbel fishing on the River Ribble in Lancashire. It's a stunning river which has a good head of barbel amongst other species and even though I was a very experienced angler, my first year was not so good to say the least. Then I caught my first barbel, "The Prince of the River" and was immediately hooked!

It played on my mind as to why my season hadn't gone quite to plan. I asked myself was it rigs, bait!? I persevered, learned and over the closed season, watching them in the clear water, I realised that if you find them and get them confident, they will eat pretty much anything! I learnt a lot over that closed season and was ready and prepared for a magic day! I quickly realised that the missing piece to the puzzle was location. I wasn't fishing the correct water for them and from that point, things changed.

The second season saw me bank 184 barbel, made up of 18 doubles, one of which is still my River Ribble PB of 14.2lb. Once I felt I mastered the Ribble, I began to try others, like the River Dove and River Trent. This brought me great success. The key thing with the barbel is location. In the summer I look for fast, pacey water with good clean gravel bottom. My rule of thumb is walking pace. In the winter I target the deeper water.

Winter fishing for barbel is all about conditions. Low pressure, milder conditions etc. Pick the right conditions and even in the deepest of winter the results can be mind blowing. I always carry a thermometer to take the water temperature. The reason for this is, conditions may look perfect but, especially in winter, if the water temp is dropping even slightly it's going to be tough going. If the temperature is rising the fishing can be very fruitful! When the temperature is rising the barbel's senses kick in and more often than not this triggers the instinct to feed.

Again, location is key, especially in winter because when the river is carrying extra flood water, the barbel will sit out of the main flow. Also, areas of slack water are very often where the barbel are more likely to be sat in big snags, i.e. trees, boulders, which can't be seen in flood. If you find these when the water is low, make a note, as these areas can often become a banker when the water is high. One of my favourite flood water pegs on the Ribble is where there is a huge boulder the size of a car! You would not see it in high water but in low water it's clearly visible, no more than 5ft from the bank. In flood conditions it's not just the barbel that sit behind it but many other species too, seeking refuge from the pacey water. I think they shelter there to get out of the fast water but also to shelter from debris that often comes hand in hand with the rising waters.

Rigs and Bait

In my fishing, simplicity is key, where rigs are concerned. I do not like to over complicate things. I only ever use free running ledger rigs whether it's a lead or feeder. I am also a massive fan of small baits for barbel. My go to baits are 6mm pellets and 10mm boilies as hookbaits. Maggots and casters play a big part in the colder months when the smaller fish are not as active. Getting bait down on your spots accurately is a key part of barbel fishing, which has been made easy for me now I have discovered a superb invention and don't leave the house without it – The Spopper.

For those of you who aren't familiar, this is a modified spomb that was invented and made by a good friend of mine, Christophe Pelhate. The spopper will be commercially available from Spomb themselves. It's basically a spomb with a weight and a pin at the front and only opens when it hits the bottom. It can be used with most baits i.e. hemp, maggots, boilies, pellets etc. Another big factor is, once you have barbel in your swim, keeping them there for longer. If you feed just boilies or 6mm pellets, they will soon clear it up and move on. To keep them I use a special mix in my spod consisting of hemp, rapeseed, chopped maize and micro pellets with plenty of fish sauce – readily and cheaply available from supermarkets and the barbel love the stuff! Another good additive to use is garlic powder! A bed of this mix can't be resisted by the barbel all year round, they go mad for it, routing through the gravel until they find every last bit. This keeps them around for longer and the garlic and fish sauce draw's them in from way downstream.

My love affair with the mighty Trent started 4 years ago I fancied a change of river and the Trent was my choice of venue, mainly the tidal stretches. I saw it as the barbel mecca of rivers having seen all of these huge barbel coming from this great river. With very little knowledge of the river Trent, I had to do my homework! I found that a great way to research the river was using google earth. It's a good way of finding spots, bends and deeper runs. After my homework was done and speaking to a few people I know, my first session was planned and it was going to be a challenge! I had only fished the smaller rivers such as the Ribble, Dove and Dane and my first session took me to the infamous Collingham stretch. I took a good drive around and a walk down the stretch and the river looked baron. I could see no obvious features as the deep water made it difficult to locate what was hidden beneath. It was also my first time seeing the infamous Cromwell Weir and it took my breath away and knew that this was now on my bucket list of where I wanted to fish!

After much deliberation I decided to fish Peg 71 on a big sweeping bend. I got set up. 4oz lead and a PVA bag on one rod and a 4oz open end feeder on the other. Both cast 3 quarters of the way across. Unfortunately, this session did not go to plan at all. Only 2 fish banked and lost 6, I concluded that my 10lb Maxima hook links were not up to the job as the fish were cutting me off on the rocks – not a great start to my Trent barbel fishing!

The bug was there from then on but, a rethink and a step up in tackle would be needed if I was to master this river. My next visit to the Trent was as a guest on the infamous Cromwell Weir. As I said earlier it was on my bucket list and this was my chance to make it great. We went into the draw and I drew Peg 1A. This was probably the most famous barbel peg in the country at the time. 20 spoppers of my spod mix went in over 2 spots and it didn't take long for the barbel to take the bait! Ten minutes after the rods went in, I had my first barbel. In the net she went and at 11.12lb she was my very first Trent double! I was hooked on the river now even more than ever.

In that first 48 hours on the Cromwell Weir saw me bank 69 barbel, 19 of which were doubles reaching up to the biggest at 14.1lb. My P.B's were broken many times in that one session. Although I was elated, I was shattered... tired was an understatement! Although I loved every minute of fishing the weir and I knew my rigs and tackle were now up to scratch, this was when I set my goals on catching these big fish throughout the tidal Trent and in no way, did I think it would be easy. I set my targets for the years to come.

I would keep heading down stream of the weir in search of bigger barbel. I continued that season fishing various and many different swims all the way along Collingham, mapping swims and catching quite consistently. I fished the Trent through the winter, with plenty of success and the only thing I changed through the winter season was the size of my hook baits. I changed from 12 and 14mm pellets and 14mm boilies to glued on 4mm pellets and 10mm boilies. This was the turning point for me. I had caught well but at this stage, with 180 barbel, 69 of which of which were caught on the weir, I still wasn't happy as most of the others were caught in the winter and the banks were quieter.

The next season I decided to target the Trent from August through until March as I felt that this would give me the best chance to get amongst the bigger barbel through these months. This season was destined to be my best season ever and was very special. I finished this season with 204 barbel, 87 of these being in the double figures, 2 of which were 14lb plus. The season also gave me a PB of 14.4 along with six 6lb chub and my first ever 7lb chub at 7.2lb. I was over the moon to say the least! My plan worked a treat but, I still wanted a 15lb Barbel or even a 16! That was then my target for the current season. I planned on the same tactics, bait and the same months but I would be heading to new stretches too. Then things changed... the terrible conditions and drought through the summer of 2018 saw me decide not to fish for them until the temperatures dropped or we had some rain. This saw me not start my campaign until mid September.

This current season from September to date has been a very special season, to say the least. My aim was to catch a 15lb barbel but to catch 2 in one night at 15.2lb and 15.12 plus a 6.15lb chub AND a PB chub of 7.7lb is something I only dreamed of and a night I will cherish forever! I've also managed 3 chub over the magic 7lb barrier which, as far as I know is unheard of in one season! And if that wasn't enough, on the coldest night of the year and when I least expected a bite, let alone a barbel, I had a take at 1.30 in the morning and managed to slip the net under a giant of a barbel at 16.2lb. I was blown away! My simple but effective rigs, the choice to take a step down in bait sizes, learning where the fish are and swim selection, particularly in winter, have all been the key to my success! I can honestly say that I have loved every minute of my experiences, particularly on the Trent and I still have a few weeks to go!

Fishing for Canal Zander

Anthony Wood

Zander is a predatory species that you may or may not have seen or even heard of. Centralised around the Midlands but with pockets around the country, the zander is a fantastic sports fish which gets demonised unfairly.

Zander have been in our country since 1878 and there are lots of arguments about when they made their way into our rivers and canals but the consensus is at least 40-50 years ago. Yet, this is a species that still hasn't been naturalised and given the same protection that other native species have. When you consider that carp aren't originally a native species, you have to wonder if zander brought more money in from anglers would they get naturalised as quick as the carp did?

Currently zander are regularly electro-fished by the powers that be which leaves a lot of the smaller zander fry, this actually creates a bigger zander problem as zander are cannibalistic and actually prefer eating smaller zander if they are available. By removing the larger zander there are no longer larger fish to keep the smaller zander numbers in check, this actually creates a boom in the zander population who in turn eat other species of fish (and signal crayfish) giving them a bad name.

Okay so how do you go about targeting this predator species? There are probably lots of ways but I would like to show you two ways that work very well for me (I've had over 350 zander in 4 years).

The first method that I'd like to show you is deadbaiting. There are a few ways to do this but I like to use a float leger rig which I will talk through first, the rig consists of a Fladen Inline sea float, a 1oz-2oz Pallatrax Stonze, a 3"-4" wire trace (make this 18" if there is a chance of a pike in the area), a Pallatrax 2/0 Eagle Wave Catfish Gripz Hook and finally a stop knot up the mainline. You want to set the stop knot so that it allows the inline float to lie flat on the surface of the water and when you get a take the float will pop up and start moving.

When deadbaiting for zander I like to use a rod such as a 1.75lb barbel rod or feeder rod, bait wise I prefer to use roach sections, in particular the head with the hook pierced through the bottom of the head coming out of the top in between the eyes.

If I don't know the section that I am fishing then I will look to cast into natural holding areas such as overhanging trees, water inlets, turning bays, marina entrances (but please be respectful of the boaters) and also I never forget the margins under my feet, it's amazing the amount of times I've had a take from almost literally right underneath me.

When you get a take, wait for the float to properly start moving and then count to 5 before striking into the take, playing the fish is fairly straightforward once hooked keep a steady pressure on and you may find that you will get a couple of runs before the fish gives up and you have a stunning looking zander in the net.

The next method I like to use is dropshotting, this method has probably accounted for over 70% of my fish as it is quick, convenient and you don't need to carry much equipment with you. To make the dropshot rig you will need a lighter rod such as the Spro Freestyle Skills Micro Lure in

3-14g or Fladen Vantage Dropshot which is slightly heavier at 7-28g but still light enough to register the tiniest of bites.

As your mainline you want a nice fine braid such as the Savage Gear Finezze HD4 13lb or the Spro Dynafil 0.08mm (6kg). You then want a fluoro hook link I use Pallatrax Fluorocarbon hook link in 15lb or Stroft FC2. Hook wise I either use a size 2 Pallatrax wide gape Gripz or a Kamasan B980 combined with a 3-5g dropshot weight and a 2-4" soft plastic lure.

So how do you dropshot? Well there are actually two methods, the first method is vertical dropshotting which is usually done from a boat and literally you put your rod out over the edge, let your rig drop to the bottom and gently lift and lower the tip of your rod so that the weight just lifts of the lake bottom and then settles back down, this creates a movement in your lure which any predator fish near find hard to resist. With the vertical lift method, it isn't unusual to have longer tails to your rigs as it is often fished in deeper water and you want your lure higher in the water.

The second method is horizontal dropshotting and is very similar to jigging in the sense that you cast your lure out and then holding your rod tip quite high slowly retrieve your lure giving the rod an occasional twitch to lift the weight off the bottom (instead of your jig) again creating a movement in your lure that predators struggle to leave alone.

This method is more often used on canals and small lakes from the bank and is ideal for placing your lure at a certain depth instead of bouncing it off the bottom. Obviously, you can use the vertical dropshot method in the margins which will quite often produce a bite.

Making the dropshot rig can seem a bit tricky to start with but once you've done it a few times it is really very easy and quick to do. Take your line and slide it through the eye of the hook making sure that the point of the hook is facing upwards from what will be the bottom of your rig, leaving around 18 inches of line at the bottom.

Next bring the bottom part of your rig around in a loop behind the hook, loop the hook through the hoop of line that you have created about 4 or 5 times and then pull tight. Now about 6-12 inches from the bottom of the hook place either two SSG shots or the dropshot weight.

So that is the rig made now it is time for you to choose the lure you want to use. This is not as simple as it sounds as there is such a huge selection of lures available in the 1 - 4-inch range. The choice really is yours but have a look at Spro and Relax to give you an idea of where to start.

There are a few ways you can connect your line to your rig, tucked half-blood knots, etc but one of the most popular is the double uni-knot.

With both the dropshot and the deadbait methods you want to travel as light as possible as a roving method works best with both styles of fishing as you will need to find the zander and once you have found them you stand a good chance of getting four or five bites as they will quite often be shoaled up together.

Make sure you have a suitable landing net, an unhooking mat and a pair of long nose forceps in case you need to remove a deep hooked lure.

As a last note I have heard and seen so many people say that you won't catch zander in sunlight or that you won't catch them in chocolate coloured water, etc, etc. I can honestly say I have caught zander in chocolate coloured water, in gin clear water, in bright sunlight and in pitch darkness. I've caught zander when it's hot and when it's cold so please don't be discouraged by people saying you won't catch them. The trick is to keep mobile until you find the zander and be patient.

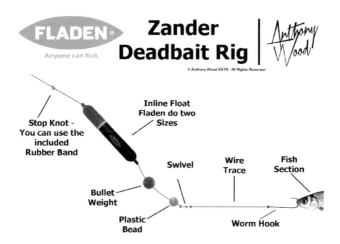

FLADEN®
Anyone can fish.

Zander Deadbait Rig

© Anthony Wood 2016 · All Rights Reserved

Stop Knot -
You can use the
included
Rubber Band

Inline Float
Fladen do two
Sizes

Bullet
Weight

Plastic
Bead

Swivel

Wire
Trace

Fish
Section

Worm Hook

Trophy shots are a fantastic way of remembering your capture but as zander are currently a persecuted species please try to hide the location of your capture as much as possible. Stand with a bush against your background or a wall or some other none descript background, if it isn't possible to hide your location then please blur your background before sharing on social media (unless of course the location is already regularly electro fished in which case it's pointless hiding the location as the powers that be already know there is a zander population there)

Above all enjoy your zander fishing and let's make this fantastic species a popular sport fish and bring it to the limelight and help it get the naturalised protection it deserves.

Printed in Great Britain
by Amazon